Shabbat Hands

*To S.J.L.,
who made this book possible*

Shabbat Hands
Written by Ken Bresler ~ Illustrated by Avi Katz

ISBN: 978-1-956381337
Copyright © 2023

Mazo Publishers
www.mazopublishers.com
info@mazopublishers.com

– All Rights Reserved –

This publication may not be translated, reproduced, stored in a retrieval system, or transmitted in any form or by any means, electronic, mechanical, photocopying, recording, imaging or otherwise, without prior permission in writing from the publisher.

Shabbat Hands

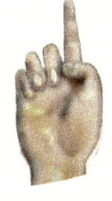 Shabbat Candles

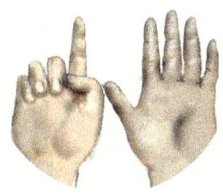 Sh'ma

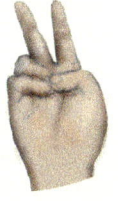 Children's Blessing

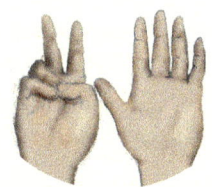 Torah

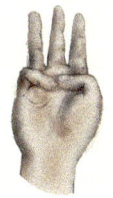 Washing Hands

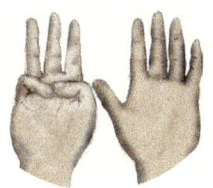 Priestly Blessing

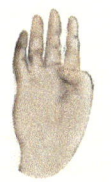 Mezuzah

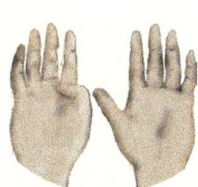 After Shul

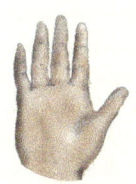 Hamsa

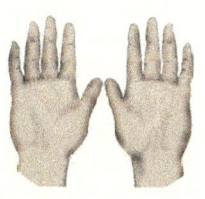 Havdalah

Ima lights the Shabbat candles, sweeps her hands around them, and covers her eyes with her hands.

Shabbat Shalom!

Abba puts his hands on our heads and blesses us. It is a special time.

We wash our hands before eating challah. We use a special pitcher with two handles.

When we leave home in the morning to go to shul, Ima and Abba touch the mezuzah, and then kiss their fingertips. They lift us so that we can do it too.

In shul, Ima wears a hamsa, jewelry shaped like a hand.

When we sing the Sh'ma, we cover our eyes with our hands to concentrate on this important prayer.

When we read from the Torah, we use a silver pointer shaped like a hand.

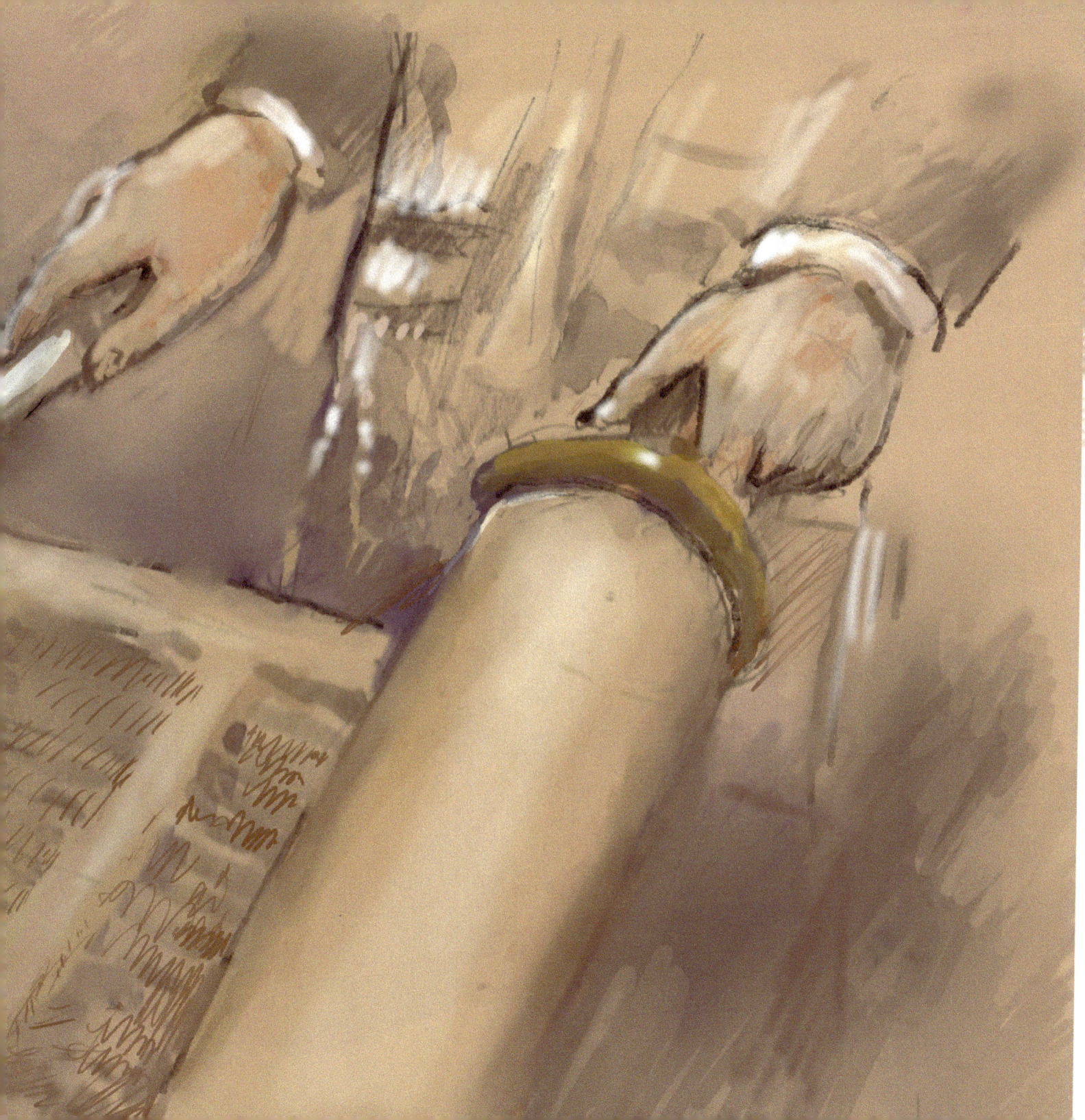

On top of the Aron, where we keep the Torah, is a pair of hands. A long time ago, in the Temple in Jerusalem, the priests held their hands this way to bless Jews.

When we leave the shul after services, Abba shakes hands with his friends. They say "Shabbat Shalom!" or "Good Shabbos!"

After Shabbat ends, we light the Havdalah candle and look at our fingernails.

Goodbye, Shabbat, till next week!

Shavuah Tov!

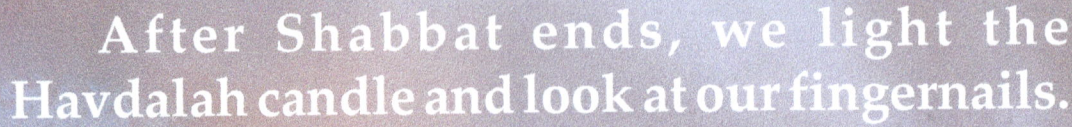

www.ingramcontent.com/pod-product-compliance
Lightning Source LLC
Chambersburg PA
CBHW041433040426
42450CB00022B/3479